GW00808314

Frances Lincoln Limited
74-77 White Lion Street,
London N1 9PF
www.franceslincoln.com

Travel Organiser and Notebook
Copyright © Frances Lincoln Limited 2014
All photographs copyright © Chris Caldicott 2014

A catalogue record for this book is available
from the British Library

Designed by Arianna Osti

ISBN 978-0-7112-3548-9

Printed in China

9 8 7 6 5 4 3 2

Back cover (clockwise from top right)
Hoshinoya Ryokan, Arashiyama, Kyoto, Japan; Syria; Dhaka, Bangladesh;
Hippos, Chobe River, Caprivi Strip, Namibia; Wat Si Saket, Vientiane, Laos
Endpapers Los Flamencos National Reserve, Laguna Chaxa, Salar de Atacama, Chile
Half-title page On the road to Paso Sico, crossing the Andes from Chile to Argentina

USING THIS BOOK

Every journey needs some organisation and, with a little planning before you set out, valuable time can be saved when you are en route. This Organiser & Notebook is the ideal place to plan and list your travel arrangements – train times, flight numbers and other essential information – together with recommendations for places to visit, stay or eat, gathered from friends or guidebooks. Using this book, your time can be as carefully planned or as spontaneous as you wish.

The unlined section is the place to write about your experiences or to make sketches of the places you explore: the sights and sounds, the unfolding landscapes, the people you meet and the discoveries you make along the way.

At the back of the book, you will find conversion tables and useful information about countries you may visit or pass through. There is space to take down the details of those you meet and tear-off notes to share information.

Sossusvlei Desert, Namibia

PLANNER

april

may

june

PLANNER

july

august

september

PLANNER

october

november

december

BUDGETS

date	details	amount	

BUDGETS

date	details	amount	

BUDGETS

date	details	amount	

BUDGETS

date	details	amount	

BUDGETS

date	details	amount	

BUDGETS

date	details	amount	

PLANNING & PACKING

Calchaquies Valley, near Cachi, Argentina

PLANNING & PACKING

PLANNING & PACKING

Punakha Dzong, Bhutan

ITINERARIES

date	location

date	location

Lapland

ITINERARIES

date	location

ITINERARIES

date	location

ITINERARIES

date	location

date	location

Airstrip, Kaokoland Desert, Namibia

PLACES TO VISIT

date	location

PLACES TO VISIT

date   location

PLACES TO VISIT

date   location

PLACES TO VISIT

date	location

Koraku-en Garden, Okayama, Japan

PLACES TO VISIT

date	location

PLACES TO VISIT

date	location

PLACES TO STAY

name	details

name	details

Great Umayyad Mosque, Damascus, Syria

PLACES TO STAY

name	details

name	details

PLACES TO EAT

name	details

name	details

Trinidad, Cuba

PLACES TO EAT

name	details

PLACES TO EAT

name	details

PLACES TO EAT

name   details

PLACES TO EAT

name	details

View of Hong Kong from the Peak

date   /   /

location

_____

date   /   /

location

date   /   /

location

Palmyra, Syria

date   /   /

location
_____

date   /   /

location
_____

Cuba

date   /   /

location
_____

Myanmar (Burma)

date   /   /

location

date   /   /

location
_____

date   /   /

location

Elephants, Susuwe Island Lodge, Caprivi Strip, Namibia

date   /   /

location

date   /   /

location

date   /   /

location

date   /   /

location

Bamboo forest, Arashiyama, Kyoto, Japan

date   /   /

location
_____

date   /   /

location
_____

U Bein Bridge, Mandalay, Myanmar (Burma)

date   /   /

location

date   /   /

location

date   /   /

location

date   /   /

location

Bhutan

date / /

location

Banks of the Padma River, Rajshahi, Bangladesh

date   /   /

location

Wat Si Saket, Vientiane, Laos

date   /   /

location

date   /   /

location
_____

date / /

location

_____

Buddhist prayer flags above the Paro Valley, Bhutan

date   /   /

location

date   /   /

location

Puthia, Rajshahi, Bangladesh

date   /   /

location

date   /   /

location

date   /   /

location

Finland

date   /   /

location

date / /

location

Banks of the Padma River, Rajshahi, Bangladesh

date   /   /

location

date   /   /

location

Palmyra, Syria
Following pages San Pedro de Atacama, Chile

TIME ZONES

-11 Samoa

-10 Hawaii/ Tahiti

-09 Alaska

-08 Pacific Time (US & Canada)

-07 Arizona/ Mountain Time (US & Canada)

-06 Mexico City/ Central Time (US & Canada)

-05 Bogota/ Lima/New York

-04 La Paz/ San Juan/ Santiago

-03 Brasilia/ Buenos Aires/ Montevideo

-02 Mid-Atlantic

-01 Azores/ Cape Verde Is.

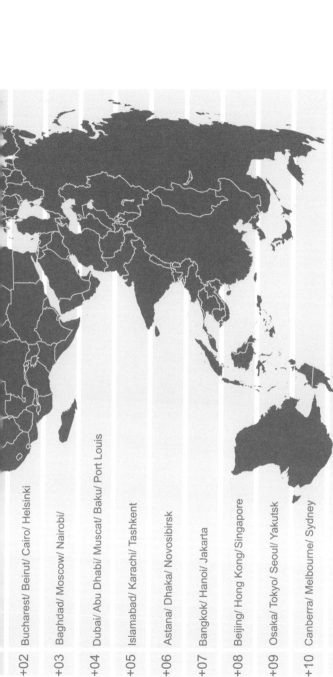

+02 Bucharest/ Beirut/ Cairo/ Helsinki

+03 Baghdad/ Moscow/ Nairobi/

+04 Dubai/ Abu Dhabi/ Muscat/ Baku/ Port Louis

+05 Islamabad/ Karachi/ Tashkent

+06 Astana/ Dhaka/ Novosibirsk

+07 Bangkok/ Hanoi/ Jakarta

+08 Beijing/ Hong Kong/ Singapore

+09 Osaka/ Tokyo/ Seoul/ Yakutsk

+10 Canberra/ Melbourne/ Sydney

+11 Magadan/ Solomon Is.

+12 Auckland/ Wellington/ Fiji

COUNTRY DIALLING CODES

country	dialling code	country	dialling code
Afghanistan	93	Dominican Republic	1809 and 1829
Albania	355	Ecuador	593
Algeria	213	East Timor	670
American Samoa	1684	Egypt	20
Andorra	376	El Salvador	503
Angola	244	Equatorial Guinea	240
Anguilla	1264	Eritrea	291
Antarctic Aust. Terr.	672	Estonia	372
Antigua and Barbuda	1268	Ethiopia	251
Argentina	54	Falkland Islands	500
Armenia	374	Faroe Islands	298
Aruba	297	Fiji	679
Ascension Island	247	Finland	358
Australia	61	France	33
Austria	43	French Guiana	594
Azerbaijan	994	French Polynesia	689
Bahamas	1242	Gabon	241
Bahrain	973	Gambia	220
Bangladesh	880	Georgia	995
Barbados	1246	Germany	49
Belarus	375	Ghana	233
Belgium	32	Gibraltar	350
Belize	501	Greece	30
Benin	229	Greenland	299
Bermuda	1441	Grenada	1473
Bhutan	975	Guadeloupe	590
Bolivia	591	Guam	1671
Bosnia-Herzegovina	387	Guatemala	502
Botswana	267	Guinea	224
Brazil	55	Guinea-Bissau	245
Brunei	673	Guyana	592
Bulgaria	359	Haiti	509
Burkina Faso	226	Honduras	504
Burma	95	Hong Kong	852
Burundi	257	Hungary	36
Cambodia	855	Iceland	354
Cameroon	237	India	91
Canada	1	Indonesia	62
Cape Verde	238	Iran	98
Cayman Islands	1345	Iraq	964
Central African Republic	236	Ireland	353
Chad	235	Israel	972
Chile	56	Italy	39
China	86	Ivory Coast	225
Christmas Island	61	Jamaica	1876
Colombia	57	Japan	81
Comoros	269	Jordan	962
Congo	242	Kazakhstan	7
Cook Islands	682	Kenya	254
Costa Rica	506	Kiribati	686
Croatia	385	Kuwait	965
Cuba	53	Kyrgyz Republic	996
Cyprus	357	Laos	856
Czech Republic	420	Latvia	371
DR Congo	243	Lebanon	961
Denmark	45	Lesotho	266
Diego Garcia	246	Liberia	231
Djibouti	253	Libya	218
Dominica	1767	Liechtenstein	423

country	dialling code	country	dialling code
Lithuania	370	St Lucia	1758
Luxembourg	352	St Pierre and Miquelon	508
Macao	853	St Vincent and the	
Macedonia	389	Grenadines	1784
Madagascar	261	Samoa	685
Malawi	265	San Marino	378
Malaysia	60	São Tomé and Principe	239
Maldives	960	Saudi Arabia	966
Mali	223	Senegal	221
Malta	356	Serbia and Montenegro	381
Marshall Islands	692	Seychelles	248
Martinique	596	Sierra Leone	232
Mauritania	222	Singapore	65
Mauritius	230	Slovakia	421
Mayotte	262	Slovenia	386
Mexico	52	Solomon Islands	677
Micronesia	691	Somalia	252
Moldova	373	South Africa	27
Monaco	377	South Korea	82
Mongolia	976	Spain	34
Montenegro	382	Sri Lanka	94
Montserrat	1664	Sudan	249
Morocco	212	Suriname	597
Mozambique	258	Swaziland	268
Myanmar	95	Sweden	46
Namibia	264	Switzerland	41
Nauru	674	Syria	963
Nepal	977	Taiwan	886
Netherlands	31	Tajikistan	992
Netherlands Antilles	599	Tanzania	255
New Caledonia	687	Thailand	66
New Zealand	64	Togo	228
Nicaragua	505	Tokelau	690
Niger	227	Tonga	676
Nigeria	234	Trinidad and Tobago	1868
Niue	683	Tunisia	216
Norfolk Island	672	Turkey	90
Northern Marianas	1670	Turkmenistan	993
North Korea	850	Turks and Caicos Islands	1649
Norway	47	Tuvalu	688
Oman	968	Uganda	256
Pakistan	92	Ukraine	380
Palau	680	United Arab Emirates	971
Palestinian Authority	970	United Kingdom	44
Panama	507	United States of America	1
Papua New Guinea	675	Uruguay	598
Paraguay	595	Uzbekistan	998
Peru	51	Vanuatu	678
Philippines	63	Venezuela	58
Poland	48	Vietnam	84
Portugal	351	Virgin Islands (UK)	1284
Puerto Rico	1787	Virgin Islands (US)	1340
Qatar	974	Wallis and Futuna	681
Réunion	262	Yemen	967
Romania	40	Yugoslavia	381
Russian Federation	7	Zambia	260
Rwanda	250	Zimbabwe	263
St Helena	290		
St Kitts and Nevis	1869		

MEASURES & CONVERSIONS

centimetres to inches

cm		inches
2.54	1	0.39
5.08	2	0.79
7.62	3	1.81
10.2	4	1.57
12.7	5	1.97
15.2	6	2.36
17.8	7	2.76
20.3	8	3.15
22.9	9	3.54
25.4	10	3.94
27.9	11	4.33
30.5	12	4.72

celsius to fahrenheit

ºc	ºf
-10	14
-5	23
0	32
5	41
10	50
15	59
20	68
25	77
30	86
35	95
40	104
45	113
50	122

metres to feet

metres		feet
0.30	1	3.3
0.61	2	6.6
0.91	3	9.8
1.22	4	13.1
1.52	5	16.4
1.83	6	19.7
2.13	7	23.0
2.44	8	26.2
2.74	9	29.5
3.05	10	32.8

litres to gallons

litres		gallons
4.5	1	0.22
9.1	2	0.44
13.6	3	0.66
18.2	4	0.88
22.7	5	1.10
27.3	6	1.32
31.8	7	1.54
36.4	8	1.76
40.9	9	1.98
45.5	10	2.20

kilometres to miles

km	miles
10	6.2
20	12.4
30	18.6
40	24.9
50	31.1
60	37.3
70	43.5
80	49.7
90	55.9
100	62.1

kilograms to pounds

kg		lb
0.45	1	2.2
0.91	2	4.4
1.36	3	6.6
1.81	4	8.8
2.27	5	11.0
2.72	6	13.2
3.18	7	15.4
3.63	8	17.6
4.08	9	19.8
4.54	10	22.0

men's suits and overcoats

American	British	Continental
36	36	46
38	38	48
40	40	50
42	42	52
44	44	54

women's suits and dresses

American	British	Continental
6	8	36
8	10	38
10	12	40
12	14	42
14	16	44
16	18	46
18	20	48

men's shoes

American	British	Continental
7.5	7	41
8.5	8	42
9.5	9	43
10.5	10	44
11.5	11	45
12.5	12	46

women's shoes

American	British	Continental
6.6	4	37
7.5	5	38
8.5	6	39
9.5	7	40
10.5	8	41

men's shirts

American	British	Continental
14	14	36
$14^{1}/_{2}$	$14^{1}/_{2}$	37
15	15	38
$15^{1}/_{2}$	$15^{1}/_{2}$	39
16	16	41
$16^{1}/_{2}$	$16^{1}/_{2}$	42
17	17	43

Cuba

Street scene, Trinidad, Cuba

STAYING IN TOUCH

STAYING IN TOUCH